Dogs

The New Anubis

All along the moorland road a caravan there comes
Where the piping curlew whistles and the brown snipe drums;
And a long lean dog
At a sling jig-jog,
A poacher to his eyelids, as all the lurcher clan,
Follows silent as a shadow, and clever as a man.

His master on the splash-board, oh, of ancient race he is;
He came down out of Egypt, as did all the Romanys;
With a hard hawk face
Of an old king race,
His hair is black and snaky, and his cheek is brown as tea,
And pyramids and poacher-dogs are made by such as he.

Now the dog he looks as solemn as the beak upon the bench,
But he'll pounce and pick a hare up, and he'll kill it with a
  wrench,
Or he'll sneak around a rick
And bring back a turkey chick;
And you'll wonder how they got all his cock-a-leerie fakes.
Well, his master comes of people who turn walking sticks
  to snakes!

There was once a god in Egypt, when the gods they first began,
With the muzzle of a lurcher on the body of a man;
But the Pharaoh of to-day
He has changed the ancient way,
And has found him a familiar by his caravan to jog
With the head piece of a Solomon, the body of a dog!

Patrick C Chalmers

but it is probable that they were of a Spitz type, with a wedge-shaped head, pricked ears and a bushy tail, similar to their wild relatives. Dogs of this type appear to have long had a world-wide distribution.

The civilizations of the Middle East bred dogs with some care and selectivity, when the more primitive peoples of the north were still at a much earlier stage of development. Egyptian murals, from 4000 B.C. onwards, show domestication of several different types of greyhounds. One has a big upright bat ear like the modern Ibizan hound, while another has the small drop ear and the feathering of the modern Saluki. It is possible that a greyhound of some type, such as the Afghan, reached Afghanistan along the trade routes of the ancient world between the Middle

Above left: This picture from the Middle Ages shows the type of spaniel used to find game for hawks. Falconry was a fashionable pursuit for both sexes.

Left: The Welsh Springer Spaniel is a good working gundog on both land and water and is active and energetic.

East and China. It was discovered there by British Army Officers in the late nineteenth century, thereafter to be introduced to the western world.

The greyhound family were at their most successful in desert countries, where the hot, still air makes for bad scenting conditions, but excellent visibility. This suits all types of greyhounds, since they hunt by sight rather than scent and use speed to overtake their prey. For this reason, they are also known as gazehounds.

Early Assyrian wall paintings also portray a much larger, heavier dog with a blunt muzzle, reminiscent of a Mastiff. These were apparently used for hunting lions and were also taken into battle by their Assyrian masters. Dogs of this type may have reached Britain with the Phoenician traders who came for Cornish tin, bringing greyhounds and mastiffs with them. The Romans discovered the British Mastiff when they invaded this island and were so impressed by its size and ferocity that they sent several back to Rome to take part in the colourful gladiatorial displays.

The Middle Eastern peoples never

seem to have bred the hounds that hunt by scent, and indeed they would have no need for such animals. The scent hound evolved in cooler, milder climates, where the thickness of the vegetation would prevent a gazehound from seeing the game. The humidity of the countries further north provided good scenting conditions for dogs bred to follow a trail with the tenacity of purpose that would enable them to wear down their quarry. From the time of the peak of Greek civilization through to the European Middle Ages, hunting with packs of scent hounds was a passion with the nobility and its importance is reflected in the complicated and punitive game laws of this period.

Spaniel-type dogs are shown in use in mediaeval times finding and putting up birds for the sport of hawking and falconry, or pointing and flushing game into nets. From these animals, many of today's well-known gundog breeds are descended.

Not all dogs were valued solely for their usefulness, however. Toy dogs have always appealed to man and the mummified remains of very small dogs have been found in Egyptian tombs. The Chinese also bred small, flat-faced dogs from early times. The first of these to reach Europe was the Pug, brought by the Dutch and Portuguese who traded with Canton in the sixteenth century and considered the small dogs valuable curiosities. The breed reached Britain from Holland with the court of William of Orange and became a fashionable lady's dog.

Many of the working breeds of the past, as opposed to the hunting dogs, have an undocumented history, for they did not attract the attention of artists or writers. We know that the vermin-hunting terriers, the cattle-droving dogs and the sheepdogs have been in existence for centuries, but we know little about their appearance before the nineteenth century. Life would not have been possible in the Arctic until very recently without the use of the dog as a haulage animal. Draught dogs were also used in many other parts of the world and we know very little about these, too.

Although some dogs have been bred with care for specific purposes over many centuries, it was not until the advent of dog shows and the formation of the Kennel Club that pedigrees as records of ancestry became the universal general practice. The only dogs whose named ancestors are known before this are some packs of Foxhounds whose stud books go back to the eighteenth century. The first organized dog show in the world was held in Britain in 1858. Its success and popularity led to the formation of the Kennel Club in 1873. The Club's first positive action was to organize a stud book and only dogs registered in this were allowed to enter the shows which it then proceeded to organize. The purpose of this was to eliminate some of the unscrupulous malpractices and anarchy that reigned at the early shows. Nowadays, the Club exists mainly for the purpose of promoting dog shows, field trials, working trials, obedience tests and the overall improvement of dogs.

The transition of the role of the dog from a work animal to a pet is largely an event of the twentieth century. Before then, really the only dogs kept as pets were the various toy breeds, which have always been bred mainly as companions. Just why the dog became accepted into society primarily as a pet is hard to say; it may have been that as families became smaller, there became a greater need to keep animals as companions to counteract the loneliness induced by smaller family units.

Below: *Toy dogs have always had an appeal for man. Pugs are sturdy little dogs, originating from the Far East where the Chinese specialized in producing small dogs with flattened muzzles to be constant companions.*

Right: *The Old English Mastiff has a long and rather bloodthirsty history. The modern breed is a giant heavyweight with a dignified character.*

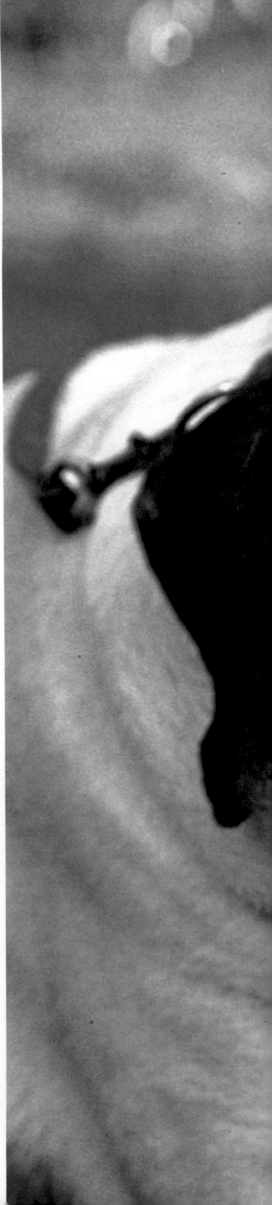

The modern breeds

This list features most of the breeds available in Britain today. Some of the extremely rare breeds have not been included as their numbers are already so low that they may not survive much longer. Each breed has been coded for size, exercise requirements, coat care and popularity (and therefore, availability) – factors which may help you to decide whether it is a suitable dog for you to keep.

The codings are as follows:

Size
G giant – 40 kg (90 lbs) weight and upwards
L large – 22 kg (50 lbs) weight and upwards
M medium – 9 kg (20 lbs) weight and upwards
S small – under 9 kg (20 lbs)

Exercise
XXX maximum – at least an hour a day, half of which should be galloping free
XX moderate – half an hour a day some of which must be off the lead
X minimum – all dogs appreciate a change of scene and fresh air but these breeds can manage with just a daily game with their owners

Coat care
CCC maximum – at least a quarter of an hour's daily attention
CC moderate – a quarter of an hour twice a week, but may need professional clipping or trimming at intervals
C minimum – grooming once a week

The coat colours mentioned under the different breeds in the following pages, may be defined as follows:
merle – blue-grey
wheaten – sandy

Left: *The English Pointer is a fine example of a dog bred to gallop all day. Its energy and stamina makes it unsuitable for town life and it needs considerable regular exercise.*

brindle – fawn with darker hairs intermingled
tricolour – black, white and tan
red – deep chestnut

Numerical rating
Popular – you should be able to find a puppy locally
Moderate – you may have to travel some distance to find a breeder
Rare – you will probably have to book a puppy in advance from a litter planned for the future

Afghan Hound – This is a spectacular hound of aristocratic looks and independent nature whose thick and long silky coat can be any colour. L, XXX, CCC, popular.

Airedale Terrier – The largest of the terriers, the Airedale possesses a workmanlike look and character. Its wiry coat is coloured black and tan. L, XX, CC plus trimming, moderate.

Alsatian – See German Shepherd Dog.

American Cocker Spaniel – This is one of the gundogs and although it no longer works in the field, it retains the biddable nature common to most retrieving breeds. Its thick, luxurious coat can be almost any colour. M, XX, CCC plus trimming, moderate.

Australian Terrier – This lively spirited little terrier has a sporting nature. Its short, hard coat is blue, or silver-grey, with tan markings. S, XX, C, rare.

Basenji – Originally from the Congo basin, this African hunting dog does not bark but makes plenty of other noises to compensate. Its smooth coat can be red, black, or black and tan with white markings. M, XX, C, moderate.

Basset Hound – Kept at one time in packs for hunting the hare, the Basset is really a large dog on short legs, and it needs lots of exercise and company. Its smooth coat can be almost any colour. L, XXX, C, popular.

Beagle – This is also a hare-hunting breed and it is determined, strong-

willed and energetic. Its smooth coat can be any colour except liver. M, XX, C, popular.

Bearded Collie – This is a Scottish sheepdog with plenty of energy and high spirits. Its shaggy coat can be any shade of grey or brown, usually with white markings. L, XXX, CCC, moderate.

Bedlington Terrier – The lamb-like look of this breed is accentuated by trimming and somewhat belies the breed's sporting nature. The coat colour is pale, either blue or liver. M, XX, CC plus trimming, moderate.

Belgian Shepherd Dog – Three types of this sheepdog are known in Britain – the semi-long-coated, all-black Groenendael; the semi-long-coated, mahogany Tervueren; and the smooth-coated, dark fawn Malinois. L, XXX, C, rare.

Bernese Mountain Dog – A Swiss breed which was once used for hauling small carts. The glossy black coat is set off by bright tan and gleaming white markings. G, XX, CC, rare.

Bichon Frise – This all-white dog has a long, thick, silky and loosely curled coat, which makes it look like a stuffed toy. S, X, CCC, rare.

Bloodhound – An independent-minded hound which is credited with the best scenting powers of any breed. Rather sensitive and often a one-man dog, needing an experienced owner. The smooth coat can be red, black and tan or liver and tan. G, XXX, C, moderate.

Border Collie – This is the working sheepdog of the world. The breed is fast, agile and intelligent, but can become neurotic if not given enough to do. It is usually tricolour, black or blue merle with white markings. M, XXX, CC, moderate.

Border Terrier – The size of this hardy and affectionate terrier makes it very adaptable to either town or country life. It may be red, wheaten, blue and tan. S, XX, C, moderate.

Borzoi – The alternative name of Russian Wolfhound indicates the original purpose of this breed. It is a

Left: The Afghan Hound's coat looks superb when carefully groomed but it takes regular care to keep it like this.

Right: The fierce-looking Boxer is usually very good-natured. Although docking dogs' tails is frowned upon in Britain, most Boxers have their tails docked when they are puppies.

very elegant dog whose silky coat can be any colour. G, XXX, CC, moderate.

Boston Terrier – This smart, lively American breed of terrier has a flattened muzzle and compact build. The short coat is brindle and white. S, X, C, moderate.

Boxer – The Boxer is a strong, active and very energetic dog whose cheerful exuberance needs a certain amount of discipline. The short coat can be fawn, brindle or red with white markings. L, XXX, C, popular.

Briard – A shaggy French sheepdog which has a rugged appearance and, like most sheepdogs, an intelligent and tractable nature. Its coat is dark; usually black, dark grey or fawn and whole colours are preferred. L, XXX, CCC, moderate.

Bulldog – The formidable looks of the Bulldog hide a kindly and rather 'soft' nature. The flattened face and wrinkled skin can lead to health problems. Any colour except black. L, X, C, moderate.

Bull Mastiff – This heavily-built, strong and good-tempered dog was initially bred as a guard dog, which is a role it still fulfils. The short coat can be brindle, fawn or red. G, XX, C, moderate.

Bull Terrier – A very agile and strong terrier, the Bull Terrier has a tendency to be a humorist. It is usually exceptionally good with children, but not always so good with other dogs or cats. The short coat may be all white or 'coloured', meaning white with red, fawn or brindle markings which should predominate. L XXX, C, moderate.

Cairn Terrier – This game, sprightly, short-legged terrier is full of cheek and courage. Its harsh coat does not need trimming and can be any colour except white. S, XX, C, popular.

Cavalier King Charles Spaniel – One of the largest of the 'toy' dogs, this is an attractive and active small spaniel. Its silky coat may be red and white, tricolour, black and tan or red. S, XX, C, popular.

Chihuahua – Although one of the most diminutive of all breeds, the Chihuahua is very agile and active for its size. There are two coat varieties; long-coated or smooth-coated and any colour is acceptable. S, X, C, popular.

Chinese Crested – This is the only hairless breed of dog established in Britain. Its skin is mottled in colour and there is a plume of hair on the head and tail. S, X, C, rare.

its size, this formidable-looking dog is usually excellent with people but needs firm training with other dogs. It may be brindle, red, fawn, blue or any of these colours with white. M, XX, C, moderate.

Sussex Spaniel – An active, strongly built spaniel that has a distinctive rolling gait and a rich golden liver colouring. M, XXX, C, rare.

Tibetan Spaniel – This rather aloof little dog has an obvious sense of its own importance. Its silky coat may be almost any colour. S, X, C, moderate.

Tibetan Terrier – A shaggy small herding dog from Tibet, that is usually a little wary of strangers but easy to train. It may be almost any colour. M, XX, CCC, rare.

Vizsla – The Vizsla is a good-tempered working gundog of lean muscular appearance. It has a russet gold coat. L, XXX, C, rare.

Weimaraner – This is a good working gundog that is responsive to training and adaptable to all situations. It has a unique mouse-grey colouring and amber eyes. L, XXX, C, moderate.

Welsh Corgi – See Corgi.

Welsh Springer Spaniel – An active spaniel built for speed and endurance, the silky coat of this breed is a rich chestnut colour with white. M, XXX, CC, moderate.

Welsh Terrier – This headstrong terrier needs an active and strong-willed owner! Its coat is black and tan. M, XXX, CC with trimming, rare.

West Highland White Terrier – A cheeky little dog whose harsh white coat does not pick up too much dirt. S, XX, CC with trimming, popular.

Whippet – The Whippet is a sleek, streamlined speed merchant with a gentle, yet sporting nature. It may be any colour. M, XX, C, popular.

Yorkshire Terrier – This active and compact little terrier possesses an air of self-importance. Its coat is dark steel blue and tan. The coat of a show dog requires maximum care, but that of a pet can be cut shorter if preferred. S, X, CC, popular.

Left: *The long, corded coat is the distinguishing feature of the Puli.*

Above right: *This standard Schnauzer has had its ear flaps cut to a point. This operation, which is illegal in Britain, is dictated by fashion.*

Right: *The russet gold colour is a distinctive feature of the Vizsla.*

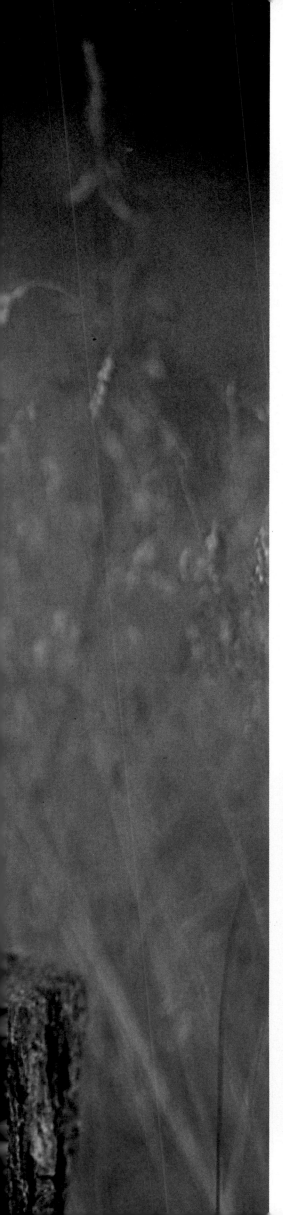

Puppyhood

Compared with the young of herbivores such as lambs and calves, puppies are born in a relatively undeveloped state. Whatever their breed, newly born puppies look very similar. All have their eyes closed and their ears folded and crumpled and they remain blind and deaf for almost the first three weeks of life. During this time they are responsive only to hunger, cold and pain. A new-born puppy's muzzle is short and blunt and its legs too small and weak to support the body weight, so that it can only crawl rather slowly. Whatever the adult coat is going to be like, the very young are covered with sleek short fur which may not necessarily be the colour of the coat in maturity.

There are differences in birth weights between breeds, of course, but these are not as great as might be expected. A puppy of a very small breed may weigh 100 g (4 oz) at birth and grow to a 2.7 kg (6 lb) adult, thus increasing its body weight 24 times. A giant breed might weigh 1 kg (2 lb) at birth and 45 kg (100 lb) when adult, an

increase of 50 times in the body weight. Proportionately, therefore, the large breeds have a lot more growing to do, and this is one of the reasons why they are slower to develop and mature. A tiny dog may be fully grown at nine months but a giant breed may not mature until two years old or more, and needs extra food for growth over a much longer period.

All mammals have a temperature-regulating mechanism which enables them to keep a constant body temperature even though the temperature of their surroundings may alter. This mechanism does not function in the newly born puppy, who can only keep warm by direct body contact with its mother. This is one of the reasons why a bitch will be very reluctant to leave a newly born litter for the first two or three days, knowing

Left: *Beagles are amongst the most popular of the hounds to keep as pets.*

Below: *These long-haired Dachshund puppies should prove to be good-natured and easy to train as they mature.*

swallowed. Large, uncooked bones provide all dogs with hours of enjoyment and help to keep teeth and gums healthy. Do not give them cooked bones which tend to splinter. Poultry, rabbit and fish bones are all especially dangerous, as they are extremely brittle.

At about four months old, the puppy teeth are pushed out by the growth of the adult set. Most puppies teethe without any trouble, though occasionally sore gums will put them off their food for a day or two. If a puppy does go off its food, make sure that it is its teeth that are the cause and that it is not actually sickening for something.

Puppies can be very rough when playing and as the puppy teeth are needle sharp, a nip or bite can be unpleasant for the owner. A bitch with a litter will growl a warning at a puppy that is biting too hard for her comfort and will then follow this with a snap if the puppy takes no notice. You, too, should prevent the puppy biting too hard by the use of the word 'No' followed by a small shake if it continues to ignore you.

Besides teaching your puppy to walk obediently by your side on a collar and lead and to answer to its name, there is one other very useful accomplishment that you can start teaching at about the age of four to five months. That is for it to lie down when you tell it to. As the dog gets older, you can build on this exercise until you have an animal that will drop flat on your command wherever it is, and will stay there until you tell it to move. The exercise can, in fact, be taught at any age, but it is easier to put a puppy in the right position on the ground than to struggle with a boisterous adult that does not understand what you are trying to achieve.

When you are teaching something new, always put the puppy on a lead so that you are in control, and always use the same word or action in connection with the particular exercise you are trying to teach. The word you use is immaterial, since all that you are attempting to do is to build an

Left: This colour of Rough Collie is called sable and white. The puppy coat lengthens as the dog matures.

Right: A Cavalier King Charles Spaniel bitch keeps a watchful eye open while her puppies sleep.

association in the dog's mind between a particular sound and a particular action. However, the word 'Flat' is probably preferable to 'Down' when teaching a dog to lie down, as the latter is liable to be used by other people should the puppy jump up at them, thereby leading to confusion. Give the command, push the puppy down into the right position and hold it there whilst praising it. Finally let it get up on your say so; 'O.K.' or 'All right' are good release words. Patient repetition at intervals of this procedure will finally result in the puppy lying down of its own accord when told. This is as far as you should go with this in a young puppy. Equally, do not be tempted to show off to other people by asking your puppy to lie down off the lead or in a place it has a choice of not obeying if it pleases. Taught slowly and carefully, this exercise can assist greatly towards having an adult dog that is always under your control, but

any attempt to rush the learning process is liable to end in unreliability and frequent disobediences throughout the dog's life.

When your dog is six months old, you will need to buy a licence for it. This can be obtained from any Post Office. From this age, too, all dogs kept in Britain must have a disc or tag giving the name and address of their owner attached to their collar. It is also the period that you can start taking your dog to a training club if you want to do so. These clubs have the advantage of trainers who are experienced in handling dogs of all types and can give advice on specific problems.

From six months to maturity (which varies from breed to breed), your dog may be likened to an adolescent who is anxious to try new experiences which may cause it to be not always as co-operative with authority as one would like!

The family dog

The dog is a highly adaptable animal in many ways and can flourish on a wide variety of diets, provided certain basic rules are observed. Dogs are carnivores – meat-eaters – so meat, or its protein equivalent, must form half to two thirds of the diet. Carbohydrates, in the form of cereal or biscuit, generally make up the rest of the meal, although some people like to add a small proportion of uncooked vegetable matter, such as raw carrot or greens. If the food is of good quality then the vitamins and minerals necessary to sustain life will already be present, and dietary supplements containing these are only necessary for the very young and old and for breeding bitches.

Left: *Dogs make the greatest companions for the young being always ready to join in with every pastime.*

Below: *Mongrel puppies can be a bit of a gamble when it comes to their looks and ultimate size.*

Fresh meat can be raw or cooked and a proportion of fat is beneficial. Meat can be replaced occasionally by fish (either filleted or pressure-cooked until the bones are soft and crumbly), cheese or eggs. Tinned dog meat, produced by a reputable manufacturer, is perfectly acceptable but check the label to see whether cereal has been added. Frozen meat must be thoroughly thawed. Commercially prepared, semi-moist foods in plastic packets are usually relished by dogs and have the advantage that, unopened, they will keep for a reasonable period; check the label to ascertain this. Dry foods, which provide a complete diet, are marketed in pellet form. These are the ultimate in convenience foods for they provide every nutritional need. All you have to do is to make sure that fresh water is always available. A dog should always have access to fresh water, but dried, complete foods, where all the water has been

than others and this is something to be borne in mind when choosing a dog. Most dogs that bark consistently do so because they are bored or lonely. Without removing the cause, you cannot expect to effect a cure. One of the easiest ways to teach a dog to stop barking on command is to say 'Quiet' and to hold its mouth shut. As with all training, though, this has to be repeated again and again with the same command and suitable praise. Only when you are perfectly satisfied that the dog understands what is wanted are you justified in correcting it if it ignores you.

Highly trained guard dogs need highly trained handlers, but many ordinary people keep a dog as some form of protection and guard. In doing this, you may run into two problems; your dog may be too protective and not allow the tradesmen to get to the front door, or, if you acquired it as an adult, it may greet everyone as a friend. In both cases, if the dog is inside when the door bell rings make it lie down a little way back from the door, but where it can see and be seen. When you open the door, the aggressive dog is therefore under your control and, from the point of view of the caller on the doorstep, the over-friendly dog in the background is an unknown quantity, which is generally sufficient deterrent in itself. If you make this a regular habit every time you answer the door, you will find that the dog will anticipate your command and take up the right position when it hears the bell. Guard against becoming careless, though, and letting the dog get up before you say it may.

Even the most highly trained working dogs need refresher training courses from time to time, so do not be afraid to go right back to square one with a dog which knew something at one time but appears to have forgotten the meaning of a command later.

Dogs, just like people, are individuals with varying amounts of initiative which they will use to their own advantage. Hopefully, if you have brought up your puppy sensibly, you will produce a well-behaved adult animal. Problems can occur, however, and since bad habits only tend to get worse, you should always seek some sort of ready solution. By training your dog you cannot alter its essential nature, but you can control undesirable behaviour. You will need patience and persistence and, above all, a strong desire to succeed. Many unruly dogs, having sized up a weak-willed owner, continue to take advantage of the situation and repeatedly get their own way.

Top dogs

The Yorkshire Terrier

This is one of the top favourites amongst the toy breeds and makes a good choice of pet for anyone who lives in a restricted space or who finds long walks difficult. The charm of the breed lies in its courage and self-importance – typical terrier attributes, but somehow particularly appealing in a dog so small. This spirited character carries a magnificent coat of dark steel blue and tan, which in the show dog sweeps the floor like a silky curtain.

The breed is not very old compared to some, having been developed mainly in the mining areas of Yorkshire during the latter half of the nineteenth century. It is not known just how the breed originated, but it is thought that various small ratting terriers were used in its development, which would account for the breed's gameness and also for the sound, workmanlike shape of the dog under its voluminous coat.

In the early days, these dogs varied greatly in size, some weighing as much as 4.5 kg (10 lbs) and some as little as 1 kg (2 lbs). They also fetched very

good prices, which doubtless encouraged many a miner's wife to rear litters of puppies in the hope of selling them at a profit to show fanciers. Such rearing conditions probably account for the sociable, affectionate nature of the Yorkie as we know it today.

The modern Yorkshire Terrier should not weigh more than 3 kg (7 lbs) and most show dogs weigh much less. However, the breed still has not stabilized completely in size. A percentage of oversize puppies are still born, and are often sold comparatively cheaply. These are often a better buy for the average owner as they are less liable to accidental injury than the

Left: The black and gold markings on this German Shepherd are one of the most popular colour combinations in this breed. The density and thickness of its coat effectively protect the dog in unfavourable weather conditions.

Below: Yorkshire Terriers vary in size, the larger animals often making better pets as they are hardier and stronger.

used as police dogs, particularly in the field of drug detection. They are also one of the mainstays for the Guide Dogs for the Blind Association, who use more Labradors and Golden Retrievers than any other breeds. They are among the most popular of family dogs, and particularly suitable for energetic, outdoor-loving households with older children. Sufficient exercise is essential and, having been bred always to fetch and carry, the breed still has a very strong desire to use their mouths. It is for this reason that bored, unhappy Labradors when shut up for long periods on their own, can sometimes be extremely destructive.

The Labrador's coat is very short and dense, and feels hard to the touch. Its slight oiliness makes it waterproof. The original Labradors were black; yellows did not appear until the beginning of this century, although they are now the favourite colour with the public. Chocolate-coloured Labradors are rare, but this is also an acceptable colour.

Grooming is simple and you need little more than a soft bristle brush. Use a bit of pressure when brushing, as this stimulates the skin and most dogs love it. A final polish with a soft duster gives a bright sheen to the coat. Combing should only be necessary when the dog is moulting.

An effective method of grooming dogs with short coats is simply to use your hands. Rake your spread fingers through the coat, working from the tail towards the neck. This will loosen dead hair and scurf and the pressure of your finger tips will stimulate the blood circulation. Finally, smooth the coat flat with the palms of your hands to give the coat gloss. The most useful piece of equipment for drying wet and muddy dogs is a large chamois leather. Wring this out tightly in hot water and rub it over the coat, squeezing out the excess water at intervals. This will clean and dry a dog to the 'just damp' stage more effectively than any other course of action.

The Labrador requires plenty of good food during its growth period. Sadly, overweight pet Labradors are all too common a sight, their owners perhaps having confused excess flesh with the sturdy build of the breed. If you are unsure whether your dog is too fat, one simple way to check is to lay your hand flat on the ribcage. If your fingers have to dig through a layer of flab to feel the bones, the dog is overweight, a condition as bad for dogs as it is for humans.

Some pet Labradors are prone to skin troubles. These are very rarely seen on the working dog, which suggests that boredom and lack of exercise might be contributory factors. The Guide Dog Association reports that skin complaints amongst the Labradors they have trained are negligible. These dogs are engaged in doing worthwhile jobs and, moreover, their blind owners have been instructed to spend half an hour a day on grooming them.

The Cocker Spaniel

Someone once said that what a Cocker Spaniel does not communicate to you with its eyes it does with its tail. This goes some way to describing the attraction of this merry, busy and charmingly friendly dog. The Cocker Spaniel was the most popular breed in Britain during the 1940s and 1950s. Twenty-seven thousand Cocker puppies were registered with the Kennel Club in 1947, a breed statistic which has yet to be equalled. Furthermore, for seventeen years, from 1936 to 1952, they were at the top of the American Kennel Club registrations, longer than any other breed. Since then the Cocker has declined numerically from these heights, but it is still a well-loved favourite with many people.

The name 'Spaniel' has been in use for several centuries, but fifteenth- and sixteenth-century illustrations show dogs that look more like small setters than the modern spaniels. The dogs were reputed to come from Spain, as the name suggests, and the early writers describe the dogs as being used to hunt for game birds and water fowl, 'setting' and 'crouching' when they scented a covey, and finally 'springing'

Left: *The American Cocker Spaniel differs from the English variety in its high domed forehead and luxurious coat.*

Below: *Cocker Spaniels have been great favourites for many years. The golden colour of these puppies is just one of the many colours found in this breed.*

the birds into the air for waiting falcons or into a net spread by the huntsman. Although spaniels then were a working 'type' rather than a breed, the merrily wagging tails, busy manner and tendency to bark that are now characteristics of the breed were all much in evidence.

Spaniels as sporting dogs continued merely to be divided into rough categories of water and land spaniels until quite late in the nineteenth century. In 1870, the Kennel Club categorized everything together under the title Field Spaniel and divided them by weight into over and under 11 kg (25 lbs). By 1893 the smaller variety had become officially called Cocker Spaniels, a name derived from the fact that they were considered particularly suitable for flushing woodcock.

The Cocker Spaniel should be built so that it is capable of doing a day's work, which involves pushing through heavy cover to find game. In other words it tends to be a compact, strong dog for its size and weight and, although few are now used for work, most pets will still hunt with tireless persistence and great enjoyment, given the opportunity. The coat is flat and silky and may be a wide variety of colours, both whole and broken with flecks or patches of white.

A medium stiff brush should be used fairly vigorously on the coat. It is particularly important to get out the dead hair, otherwise the coat looks bunchy and dry instead of flat and silkily gleaming. The feet should be neatened by trimming round them with blunt-ended scissors, and the hair should also be snipped from between the toes. This helps to keep the foot compact and prevents the dog bringing too much mud indoors with it. Thinning scissors should be used on the feathering down the back of the legs and on the tops of the ears, to prevent it becoming too profuse. Some Cocker Spaniels have a tuft of rather woolly hair on the dome of their heads and this should be gently stripped away by pulling out the hairs. This is a very sensitive part of the dog however, so be very careful.

Cockers can suffer from ear troubles and the procedure detailed for Poodles should be followed. It is worth buying a deep, narrow feeding bowl so that the dog's ears do not get covered with food at each meal. Alternatively, the ears can be tucked into an old nylon stocking to keep them out of the way when the dog is fed. Cockers love comfort and food, and those beseeching eyes and gentle velvet mouth have tempted many an unwary owner into giving too many titbits, so make sure you watch your dog's waistline carefully.

Sadly there are some snappy and irritable little Cockers about, a travesty of the true breed temperament, so always try to buy a puppy from a sweet-tempered line.

The Cocker Spaniel type was very varied in America for a long time, a situation which was resolved in 1946 by the American Kennel Club recognizing the American Cocker Spaniel as a separate and distinct breed and it is the latter which is the American favourite. These dogs are rather smaller than their English counterpart. The muzzle is shorter and the skull domed, which gives them a rather more pert expression. The most noticeable difference, however, is the wealth of coat carried by the American Cocker which may fairly be said to be dripping glamour, in some cases with hair to the floor.

The Irish Setter

This big, handsome, boisterous dog is often called the Red Setter because of its gleaming, bright chestnut coat. The breed comes from Ireland and, in common with most Irish breeds, very little is known about its origin and possible ancestry.

Setting is an old term meaning the same as pointing – that is indicating where game is hidden by pausing and staring in that direction. Setting dogs have been used at least since mediaeval times to find game birds but the heyday of the Setters in the shooting fields came in the Victorian era. The landed gentry had big estates devoted to pheasant, grouse and partridge, and these provided the space which is really needed to work Setters effectively. The dog was expected to range in front of the guns, galloping across a wide strip of ground, which it gradually quartered so that every area was searched for sitting birds. When the dog caught the air scent of the game birds on the ground it froze into the classic position of a dog pointing

Right: *The handsome, boisterous Irish Setter is popularly nicknamed the Red Setter, because of its rich golden coat.*

Exotic dogs

Man has always had an interest in the unusual and bizarre. Rarities of all sorts have commanded attention, although in some historical records it can be difficult to sift the evidence sufficiently to decide what is factual and what is hyperbolic. With regard to dogs, we do know for certain that very small or very large dogs, very aggressive or courageous ones, and those with specialized hunting abilities have always been considered valuable commodities. For centuries they were taken along the ancient trade routes of the world or sent as suitable presents from the courts of one sovereign ruler to another. Then, as now, novelty made news.

The dog is the domestic animal in which the widest variety of type exists. Dogs can vary in weight from 1 to 56 kg

Left: The glamorous Shih Tzu originally came from Tibet. The hair on the head should give a chrysanthemum-like effect to the face.

Below: The Japanese Chin is a dainty oriental toy dog.

(2 to 120 lbs), yet to the scientist they are all one species, probably descended from a common ancestor. It is difficult for the layman to understand how such wide differences of type can exist in a single species, especially since the genetic material passed on from parent to offspring is subject to very little change. Very occasionally, however, genes mutate – that is, a change occurs in the gene structure of a reproductive cell. Little is known about what causes it, although radiation is known to increase the incidence. Mutations are seldom beneficial in populations of wild animals, and the survival rate is low. However domestic dogs are a protected population, in which mutations affecting size, body shape, coat, colouring and other physical features can survive and become established as normal.

If the dog was domesticated some 10,000 years ago, then a statistical theory advanced by a geneticist decrees that only ten mutations in that period of time would give 1,024

different forms of shape and coat colour, provided each mutation affected both shape and colour. The wolf, believed to be the ancestor of the dog, also shows quite a wide variation of size and colour in the wild. It is easy to understand why there are so many breeds of dog differing so widely in size, shape and colouring.

Amongst the rarities of the dog world, it is perhaps the hairless breeds that have pride of place. It is not known what causes this condition, but hairless dogs have been quite widely distributed in the past in tropical and semi-tropical countries including Africa, Argentina, the West Indies and Mexico. A little over a century ago, hairless dogs were mentioned as being comparatively common along the Mexican–United States border and today the Mexican Kennel Club recognizes one hairless breed with the totally unpronounceable name of Kloloitzcuintli. The skin of this animal is a uniform dark bronze or elephant grey and, without the insulating covering of hair, feels hot to the touch. This fact possibly accounts for the belief in the past that these dogs had miraculous healing powers, as demonstrated in Jamaica, where hairless dogs were known as 'fever dogs' and were stretched across the body of the sufferer apparently to neutralize the fever.

The Chinese Crested Dog is the only hairless breed established in Britain, where it has a small but constant following. It is a toy breed, weighing up to 5 kg (12 lbs) and it actually has a crest of hair on the head and a plume of hair on the tail. The skin can be any colour, but is usually mottled with grey and pink, rather like the bark of a plane tree. Although it is an active and graceful little dog, its lack of coat means that not only must it be protected from the cold, but also from sunburn and any substances liable to set up skin allergies.

At the other extreme are those dogs whose length and density of coat are quite remarkable. This is particularly notable in two Hungarian breeds, the Komondor and the Puli, both of which are present in small numbers in Britain. The Komondor is a very large white dog used as a guard for the cattle and sheep that graze on the Hungarian plains. The exceptionally long and profuse coat hangs in cords and felted mats almost to the ground, thus providing almost complete protection against extremes of weather and external injury, but it is also an excellent hiding place for skin

Above and below left: The naked appearance of the Chinese Crested Dog is not to everybody's taste. However, they are quite robust and alert little dogs that have the advantage of being odourless. Despite the name no one knows quite how they originated, although hairless breeds like this one have been known and prized for many centuries. The skin can be any colour, either plain or spotted.

Right: The Puli is a nimble and agile dog with a sturdy muscular frame under that wealth of coat. Having been used as a herding dog on the Hungarian plains, the Puli is intelligent and responsive. Although renowned for being extremely independent, the Puli also makes a good 'town' pet. It is sometimes used by the police force, too, as a working dog.

parasites. These must be searched for and treated accordingly.

The Puli is a medium-sized dog with the agility and intelligence necessary to any breed whose primary work is controlling large flocks of sheep. The coat is usually black, and hangs in long cords that develop a rusty tinge as the animal becomes older. The hair totally obscures the animal's shape, and when the dog moves the hair swings like an old lady's voluminous skirts, gathering leaves and other debris. Puli owners claim, however, that looking after the coat is not a great chore. Puppies have short, fluffy hair and as this lengthens, it twists into cords which grow longer as the animal matures. Once the coat is corded, the dog cannot be brushed or combed, but it can be bathed. This is obviously a major operation and one that is unlikely to be tackled by the average owner as frequently as might reasonably be considered to be necessary and yet it is vital for hygiene and health reasons.

Neither Komondors or Pulis appear to suffer unduly in the heat, thereby providing a good illustration of the fact that hair not only insulates against extremes of cold but also protects against the effects of direct sunlight and hot weather.

Deep skin creases, such as those on the heads of Bloodhounds or Bulldogs, are even more of a feature in a breed like the Sharpeis. This dog appears to have a skin several sizes too large for its body, and it is covered by

accordian-like pleats and folds. The breed is reputed to come from China and a handful have reached the United States, although, it would seem, in too small a number to expect them to become established as a recognized or popular breed.

Amongst the toy breeds, which have been valued as amusing companions down the centuries, a number of attempts have been made to breed dogs resembling other animals. The Pekingese, the Shih Tzu and the Lhasa Apso were all endeavours to symbolize the lion of Buddha, although the lion was an animal unknown in the Chinese and Tibetan homelands of these breeds. Various small European breeds have also been referred to as lion dogs, usually because their coats were clipped in a fashion that left a mane and a tufted tail tip. The Lowchen is the modern example of this practice.

Other small dogs were valued because of their resemblance to monkeys and a number of them can be seen in paintings of the Renaissance period, often wearing belled or ornamental collars. Their modern equivalent is the Affenpinscher (the German name meaning 'monkey terrier'). This small black dog has a pair of brilliant dark eyes which sparkle with mischief and humour. These, together with its air of comic seriousness, its prominent bearded chin, moustache and beetling brows, combine to give a simian impression. It is quite a popular breed on the

Index

Acknowledgments

The publishers would like to thank the following organizations and individuals for their kind permission to reproduce the photographs in this book:

Animal Graphics 4–5, 50 below left, centre and right; Ardea London (Kenneth Fink) 9 below, (Jean Paul Ferrero) 12 below, 22, 31, 57, 65, 66–67, 81 above right, 87, (Pat Morris) 14–15, 46; Bavaria Verlag 30, 52, 70–71, 73, 86 above; Sdeuard C Bisserot 82; Bruce Coleman Ltd (Barry Davies) 36 above left; Anne Cumbers 17, 26, 37, 48, 56 above, 68, 80; Daily Telegraph Colour Library (Robert Hallmann) 25, 55; Robert Estall 10 below, 43 above, 92; Mary Evans Picture Library 16 below left; Jacana Agence de Presse 15, 16 above left, 18–19, 23, 28–29, 62, 66, 69, 74 above, 84–85, 88 below right, 93 centre; Jane Miller 24, 78–79; John Moss 11, 50 above right, 51, 54, 61, 77, 81 below right, 83; Musee de Cluny, Paris 10 above; Rex Features Ltd 40–41; Clive Sawyer 58–59 below, 76, 94; Spectrum Colour Library 72; Tony Stone Associates 20–21, 28 above, 33 above right, 42–43, 44, 45, 64, 79 below, 89; Sally Anne Thompson 1–3, 18 below, 27, 32, 33 below right, 36 below left, 38, 39, 40 above, 60, 63, 74–75, 86 below left, 88 above left, 90–91, 93 above; Shin Yoshino 49, 85 below; Zefa 35 below, 47; Zefa/Reinhard 7, 8–9, 34–35.

PDO 80-130